COOL RECIPES

Publications International, Ltd.
Favorite Brand Name Recipes at www.fbnr.com

Louis Weber, CEO
Publications International, Ltd.
7373 North Cicero Avenue
Lincolnwood, IL 60712

Recipe Development (pages 38-58): David Zino

Back cover photography and photography on pages 39, 41, 43, 45, 47, 49, 51, 53, 55, 57 and 59 by Peter Dean Ross Photographs, Inc.
Photographers: Alex Atevich, Peter Dean Ross
Prop Stylist: Carey Thornton
Food Stylists: Kim Hartman, Carol Parik
Photographers Assistant: Eric Coughlin

Pictured on the front cover *(clockwise from top left):* Country Captain Chicken *(page 50),* Curry Pasta Salad *(page 24),* Hickory Beef Kabob *(page 18)* and Fresh Fruit Trifle *(page 78).*

Pictured on the back cover *(clockwise from left):* Chocolate Raspberry Mousse Pie *(page 86),* Smoked New Potato Salad *(page 36)* and Chicken and Fruit Kabobs *(page 22).*

ISBN: 0-7853-5171-X

Manufactured in China.

8 7 6 5 4 3 2 1

Microwave Cooking: Microwave ovens vary in wattage. Use the cooking times as guidelines and check for doneness before adding more time.

CONTENTS

Coca-Cola®

DINNER ON THE GRILL

Guadalajara Beef

1 can (about 14 ounces) beef broth
¼ cup low-sodium soy sauce
3 cloves garlic, minced
1 teaspoon ground cumin
1 teaspoon chili powder
½ teaspoon ground red pepper
1 pound beef flank steak

6 medium red, yellow or green bell peppers, seeded and cut lengthwise into quarters
8 (6- to 8-inch) flour tortillas
Sour cream
Salsa

Combine beef broth, soy sauce, garlic, cumin, chili powder and ground red pepper in resealable plastic food storage bag; knead bag to combine. Add beef and seal. Refrigerate up to 24 hours, turning occasionally.

Remove beef from marinade; discard remaining marinade. Grill beef over hot coals 7 minutes per side or until desired doneness. Grill bell peppers 7 to 10 minutes or until tender, turning once.

Slice beef and serve with bell peppers, tortillas, sour cream and salsa.

Makes 4 servings

Grilled Swordfish with Hot Red Sauce

2 to 3 green onions
2 tablespoons Sesame Salt
(recipe follows)
4 swordfish or halibut steaks
(about 1½ pounds total)
2 tablespoons hot bean
paste*

2 tablespoons soy sauce
4 cloves garlic, minced
4 teaspoons sugar
1 tablespoon dark sesame oil
⅛ teaspoon black pepper

*Available in specialty stores or Asian markets.

Spray grid of grill with nonstick cooking spray. Prepare coals for grill.

Cut off and discard root ends of green onions. Finely chop enough green onions to measure ¼ cup; set aside. Prepare Sesame Salt; set aside.

Rinse swordfish and pat dry with paper towels. Place in shallow glass dish.

Combine green onions, hot bean paste, soy sauce, Sesame Salt, garlic, sugar, sesame oil and pepper in small bowl; mix well.

Spread half of marinade over fish; turn fish over and spread with remaining marinade. Cover with plastic wrap and refrigerate 30 minutes.

Remove fish from marinade; discard remaining marinade. Place fish on prepared grid. Grill fish over medium-hot coals 4 to 5 minutes per side or until fish is opaque and flakes easily with fork. Garnish as desired.

Makes 4 servings

Sesame Salt

½ cup sesame seeds   ¼ teaspoon salt

Heat small skillet over medium heat. Add sesame seeds; cook and stir about 5 minutes or until seeds are golden. Cool. Crush toasted sesame seeds and salt with mortar and pestle or process in clean coffee or spice grinder. Refrigerate in covered glass jar.   *Makes about ½ cup*

Grilled Swordfish with Hot Red Sauce

Spice-Rubbed Beef Brisket

2 cups hickory chips
1 teaspoon salt
1 teaspoon paprika
1 teaspoon chili powder
1 teaspoon garlic pepper
1 beef brisket
(3 to 3½ pounds)
¼ cup beef broth
1 tablespoon Worcestershire
sauce
1 tablespoon balsamic
vinegar

1 teaspoon olive oil
¼ teaspoon dry mustard
6 ears corn, cut into 2-inch
pieces
12 small new potatoes
6 carrots, cut into 2-inch
pieces
2 green bell peppers, cut into
2-inch squares
6 tablespoons lemon juice
1½ teaspoons salt-free Italian
seasoning

Cover hickory chips with water and soak for 30 minutes. Prepare grill for indirect grilling. Bank briquets on either side of water-filled drip pan.

Combine salt, paprika, chili powder and garlic pepper. Rub spice mixture on both sides of brisket; loosely cover with foil and set aside. Combine beef broth, Worcestershire sauce, vinegar, oil and dry mustard.

Drain hickory chips and sprinkle ½ cup over coals. Place brisket directly over drip pan; grill on covered grill over medium coals for 30 minutes. Baste and turn over every 30 minutes for 3 hours or until meat thermometer reaches 160°F when inserted in thickest part of brisket. Add 4 to 9 briquets and ¼ cup hickory chips to each side of fire every hour.

Alternately thread vegetables onto metal skewers. Combine lemon juice with 6 tablespoons water and Italian seasoning; brush on vegetables. Grill vegetables with brisket 20 to 25 minutes or until tender, turning once.

Remove brisket to cutting board; tent loosely with foil and let stand 10 minutes before carving. Remove excess fat. Serve with vegetable kabobs. Garnish as desired.   *Makes 12 servings*

Tex-Mex Pork Kabobs with Chili Sour Cream Sauce

2¼ teaspoons chili powder, divided

1¾ teaspoons ground cumin, divided

¾ teaspoon garlic powder, divided

¾ teaspoon onion powder, divided

¾ teaspoon dried oregano leaves, divided

1 pork tenderloin and cut into 1-inch pieces (1½ pounds), trimmed

1 cup sour cream

¾ teaspoon salt, divided

¼ teaspoon black pepper

1 *each* red, green and yellow bell pepper, cut into small chunks

Blend 1½ teaspoons chili powder, 1 teaspoon cumin, ½ teaspoon garlic powder, ½ teaspoon onion powder and ½ teaspoon oregano in medium bowl. Add pork. Toss well to coat. Cover tightly and refrigerate 2 to 3 hours.

Combine sour cream, remaining spices, ¼ teaspoon salt and black pepper in small bowl. Mix well. Cover tightly and refrigerate 2 to 3 hours.

If using wooden skewers, soak them in water 20 minutes before using. Prepare grill for direct cooking.

Toss pork with remaining ½ teaspoon salt. Thread meat and bell peppers onto skewers. Grill over medium-hot coals 10 minutes or until meat is no longer pink in center, turning several times. Serve immediately with sour cream sauce. *Makes 4 to 6 servings*

Honey and Mustard Glazed Chicken

1 whole chicken (4 to 5 pounds)

1 tablespoon vegetable oil

¼ cup honey

2 tablespoons Dijon mustard

1 tablespoon low-sodium soy sauce

½ teaspoon ground ginger

⅛ teaspoon black pepper

Dash salt

Prepare grill for indirect cooking.

Remove giblets from chicken cavity; reserve for another use or discard. Rinse chicken with cold water; pat dry with paper towels. Pull skin over neck; secure with metal skewer. Tuck wings under back; tie legs together with wet string. Lightly brush chicken with oil.

Combine honey, mustard, soy sauce, ginger, pepper and salt in small bowl; set aside.

Place chicken, breast side up, on grid directly over drip pan. Grill, covered, over medium-high heat 1 hour 30 minutes or until internal temperature reaches 180°F when tested with meat thermometer inserted into thickest part of thigh, not touching bone. Brush with honey mixture every 10 minutes during last 30 minutes of cooking time.*

Transfer chicken to cutting board; cover with foil. Let stand 15 minutes before carving. Internal temperature will continue to rise 5° to 10°F during stand time.   *Makes 4 to 5 servings*

If using grill with heat on one side (rather than around drip pan), rotate chicken 180° after 45 minutes of cooking time.

Grilled Meat Loaf

1½ pounds ground chuck or ground sirloin	½ teaspoon black pepper
½ cup seasoned dry bread crumbs	¼ teaspoon salt
⅔ cup chili sauce, divided	2 tablespoons packed light brown sugar
⅓ cup grated onion	1 tablespoon spicy brown or Dijon mustard
1 egg	

Prepare grill for direct cooking. Combine beef, bread crumbs, ⅓ cup chili sauce, onion, egg, pepper and salt in large bowl; mix well. On cutting board or cookie sheet, shape mixture into 9×5-inch oval loaf, 1½ inches thick.

Combine remaining ⅓ cup chili sauce, sugar and mustard in small bowl; mix well. Set aside. Place meat loaf on grid. Grill meat loaf, on covered grill, over medium-hot coals 10 minutes. Carefully turn meat loaf over using 2 large spatulas.

Brush chili sauce mixture over top of meat loaf. Continue to grill, covered, 10 to 12 minutes for medium-well or until desired doneness is reached. (If desired, insert instant-read thermometer* into center of thickest part of meat loaf. Thermometer should register 160°F for medium-well.) Let stand 10 minutes before slicing.   *Makes 4 to 6 servings*

Do not leave instant-read thermometer in meat loaf during grilling since thermometer is not heatproof.

13

Grilled Scallops and Vegetables with Cilantro Sauce

1 teaspoon hot chili oil	1 pound sea scallops
1 teaspoon dark sesame oil	2 zucchini, cut into ½-inch slices
1 green onion, chopped	
1 tablespoon finely chopped fresh ginger	2 yellow squash, cut into ½-inch slices
1 cup ⅓-less-salt chicken broth	1 yellow onion, cut into wedges
1 cup chopped fresh cilantro	8 mushrooms

Spray cold grid with nonstick cooking spray. Preheat grill to medium-high heat. Heat chili oil and sesame oil in small saucepan over medium-low heat. Add green onion; cook about 15 seconds or just until fragrant. Add ginger; cook 1 minute.

Add chicken broth; bring mixture to a boil. Cook until liquid is reduced by half. Place mixture in blender or food processor with cilantro; blend until smooth. Set aside.

Thread scallops and vegetables onto skewers. Grill about 8 minutes per side or until scallops turn opaque. Serve hot with cilantro sauce. Garnish, if desired.   *Makes 4 servings*

TIP

Store cilantro, stems down, in a glass of water in the refrigerator with a plastic bag over the leaves to prevent drying. Use only the leaves in cooking and tear them just before using to maximize flavor and nutritional content.

Grilled Greek Vegetable Dinner

½ pound eggplant, cut into
  ½-inch-thick slices
1 zucchini or yellow squash,
  cut lengthwise into
  ½-inch-thick slices
1 red onion, cut into
  ¼-inch-thick slices
1 red bell pepper, cut
  lengthwise into
  1-inch-thick strips
1 ear corn, husked and cut
  into 4 equal pieces
¼ cup olive oil

¼ cup balsamic vinegar
3 cloves garlic, chopped
3 tablespoons chopped fresh
  oregano
1 cup drained canned
  chick-peas
¼ cup buttermilk
½ teaspoon salt
½ teaspoon black pepper
½ cup (2 ounces) crumbled
  feta cheese
¼ cup pine nuts, toasted

Combine eggplant, zucchini, red onion, bell pepper and corn in large shallow dish. Combine oil, vinegar, garlic and oregano in food processor or blender; process until oregano is minced. Pour ¼ cup oil mixture over vegetables; toss gently to coat. Let stand 30 minutes.

Add chick-peas, buttermilk, salt and black pepper to remaining oil mixture in food processor; process until smooth. Refrigerate.

Arrange vegetables in lightly oiled grill basket. Cook, covered, over medium-hot coals 12 to 15 minutes or until golden and tender, turning occasionally. Transfer to shallow serving dish.

Drizzle vegetables with bean mixture. Sprinkle with feta cheese and pine nuts.   *Makes 2 servings*

TIP

Eggplant is often salted before cooking to draw off some of the bitter juices.

16

Hickory Beef Kabobs

1 pound boneless beef top
    sirloin or tenderloin
    steak, cut into 1¼-inch
    pieces
2 ears fresh corn,* shucked,
    cleaned and cut
    crosswise into 1-inch
    pieces
1 red or green bell pepper,
    cut into 1-inch squares
1 red onion, cut into
    ½-inch wedges
½ cup beef broth
½ cup chili sauce
1 teaspoon dry mustard
2 cloves garlic, minced
3 cups hot cooked white rice
¼ cup chopped fresh parsley

*Four small ears frozen corn, thawed, can be substituted for fresh corn.

Place beef, corn, bell pepper and onion in large resealable plastic food storage bag. Combine beef broth, chili sauce, mustard and garlic in small bowl; pour over beef and vegetables. Seal bag tightly, turning to coat. Marinate in refrigerator at least 1 hour or up to 8 hours, turning occasionally.

Prepare grill for direct cooking. Meanwhile, cover 1½ cups hickory chips with cold water; soak 20 minutes.

Drain beef and vegetables; reserve marinade. Alternately thread beef and vegetables onto 4 (12-inch) metal skewers. Brush with reserved marinade.

Drain hickory chips; sprinkle over coals. Place kabobs on grid. Grill kabobs, on covered grill, over medium-hot coals 5 minutes. Brush with reserved marinade; turn and brush again. Discard remaining marinade. Continue to grill, covered, 5 to 7 minutes for medium or until desired doneness is reached.

Combine rice and chopped parsley; serve kabobs over rice mixture.

Makes 4 servings

Hickory Beef Kabob

Grilled Fish with Chili-Corn Salsa

1 cup cooked corn
1 large tomato, seeded and
    diced
¼ cup thinly sliced green
    onions with tops
¼ cup canned diced green
    chilies
4 teaspoons olive oil, divided
1 tablespoon coarsely
    chopped cilantro

1 tablespoon lime juice
⅛ teaspoon ground cumin
    Salt and black pepper
1½ pounds firm-textured fish
    steaks or fillets such as
    salmon, halibut, sea
    bass or swordfish, each
    1 inch thick

Combine corn, tomato, green onions, green chilies, 2 teaspoons oil, cilantro, lime juice and cumin in small bowl; mix well. Add salt and pepper to taste. Let stand at room temperature 30 minutes for flavors to blend. Brush fish with remaining 2 teaspoons oil; season with salt and pepper. Prepare grill for direct cooking; grease grid. Place fish on grid 4 to 6 inches above solid bed of coals (coals should be evenly covered with gray ashes). Cook, turning once, 4 to 5 minutes on each side or until fish turns opaque and just begins to flake.
Makes 4 servings

High-Country Lamb

1 leg of lamb (6 to 7 pounds),
    boned and butterflied
¼ cup olive oil
¼ cup lemon juice
1 clove garlic, minced

1 teaspoon dried oregano
1 teaspoon salt
½ teaspoon black pepper
½ teaspoon ground cumin
⅛ teaspoon hot pepper sauce

Place lamb in large resealable plastic food storage bag. Combine remaining ingredients in small bowl. Pour over meat; seal bag. Refrigerate 4 to 6 hours or overnight, turning bag occasionally to distribute marinade.

Prepare grill for direct cooking; grease grid. Remove meat from refrigerator and bring to room temperature. Remove meat from marinade and drain briefly; reserve marinade. Place meat on grid 4 to 6 inches above solid bed of coals (coals should be evenly covered with gray ashes). Cook, uncovered, about 50 minutes for medium or until internal temperature reaches 145°F when tested with meat thermometer inserted into thickest part of meat. Baste frequently and turn as needed to brown evenly.

Transfer meat to cutting board; cover with foil. Let stand 10 to 15 minutes before carving. Internal temperature will continue to rise 5° to 10°F during stand time.
Makes 8 to 10 servings

Grilled Beef with Creamy Jalapeño Sauce

2 egg yolks
1 tablespoon coarsely
    chopped cilantro
1 to 1½ teaspoons chopped
    fresh or canned jalapeño
    peppers
2 tablespoons lemon juice
¾ cup butter, melted and
    warm

2 to 3 drops hot pepper sauce
6 ground beef patties, about
    1 inch thick, *or* 6 small
    New York or club steaks,
    1 inch thick
Salt
Black pepper

Blend egg yolks, chopped cilantro and jalapeño peppers in blender until seasonings are finely chopped. Heat lemon juice in small pan to simmering. Add to egg yolk mixture; blend 45 seconds. With motor on medium speed, add butter, a few drops at a time in the beginning but increase to a thin, regular stream as mixture begins to thicken. (Sauce will be consistency of a creamy salad dressing.) Stir in hot pepper sauce. Pour into jar; cover. Let stand at room temperature up to 1 hour. While meat is cooking, place jar in hot water; stir until sauce is warm, not hot.

Prepare grill for direct cooking; grease grid. Place meat on grid 4 to 6 inches above solid bed of coals (coals should be evenly covered with gray ashes). Cook, turning once, 3 to 5 minutes on each side for rare or to desired doneness. Season with salt and black pepper to taste. Spoon sauce over meat.   *Makes 6 servings*

21

TIP

To check if an egg is fresh, place it in a bowl of cold water. A fresh egg will sink, a stale egg will float.

Grilled Pork Tenderloin with Tomato Mango Salsa

2 (¾-pound) pork tenderloins
⅓ cup reduced-sodium teriyaki sauce
2 tomatoes, seeded and diced
1 cup diced mango
½ cup minced yellow or green bell pepper
¼ cup hot jalapeño jelly, melted
2 tablespoons white wine vinegar

Rub pork tenderloins all over with teriyaki sauce; let stand 5 minutes.

Combine tomatoes, mango, bell pepper, jelly and vinegar in medium bowl; mix well. Set aside.

Grill pork, covered, over medium-hot coals 20 to 25 minutes or until meat thermometer inserted in thickest part registers 160°F, turning once. Slice and serve with salsa. *Makes 6 servings*

Chicken and Fruit Kabobs

1¾ cups honey
¾ cup fresh lemon juice
½ cup Dijon mustard
⅓ cup chopped fresh ginger
4 pounds boneless skinless chicken breasts, cut up
6 fresh plums, pitted and quartered
3 firm bananas, cut into chunks
4 cups fresh pineapple chunks (about half of medium pineapple)

Combine honey, lemon juice, mustard and ginger in small bowl; mix well. Thread chicken and fruit onto skewers, alternating chicken with fruit; brush generously with honey mixture. Place kabobs on grill about 4 inches from heat. Grill 5 minutes on each side, brushing frequently with honey mixture. Grill 10 minutes or until chicken is no longer pink in center, turning and brushing frequently with remaining honey mixture.

Makes 12 servings

Coca-Cola®

SALAD DAYS AND NIGHTS

Curry Pasta Salad

6 ounces uncooked small shell pasta

1 container (6 to 8 ounces) lemon nonfat or low-fat yogurt

2 tablespoons fresh lime juice

¾ teaspoon curry powder

¼ teaspoon salt

⅛ teaspoon black pepper

1 ripe mango, peeled and cut into ½-inch pieces

1 red bell pepper, cut into ¼-inch dice

1 to 2 green onions, thinly sliced

2 tablespoons chopped cilantro

2 tablespoons chopped peanuts

Lime wedges (optional)

Prepare pasta according to package directions; drain well and set aside. Meanwhile, combine yogurt, lime juice, curry powder, salt and black pepper in medium bowl. Add pasta and stir until evenly coated with dressing.

Spoon mango over pasta. Top with bell pepper, onions and cilantro; sprinkle with peanuts. Gently mix before serving. Serve with lime wedges, if desired.

Makes 6 servings

Crab Spinach Salad with Tarragon Dressing

12 ounces coarsely flaked cooked crabmeat *or* 2 packages (6 ounces each) frozen crabmeat, thawed and drained

1 cup chopped tomato

1 cup sliced cucumber

⅓ cup sliced red onion

¼ cup nonfat salad dressing or mayonnaise

¼ cup low-fat sour cream

¼ cup chopped fresh parsley

2 tablespoons skim milk

2 teaspoons chopped fresh tarragon or ½ teaspoon dried tarragon leaves

1 clove garlic, minced

¼ teaspoon hot pepper sauce

8 cups torn washed stemmed spinach

Combine crabmeat, tomato, cucumber and onion in medium bowl. Combine salad dressing, sour cream, parsley, milk, tarragon, garlic and hot pepper sauce in small bowl. Line four salad plates with spinach. Place crabmeat mixture on spinach; drizzle with dressing. *Makes 4 servings*

Chicken-Peanut Salad

¾ cup reduced-fat mayonnaise

1 teaspoon ground cumin

1 teaspoon lemon juice

½ teaspoon onion powder

½ teaspoon salt

¼ teaspoon garlic powder

¼ teaspoon black pepper

3 cups diced cooked chicken

1 cup seedless grapes, cut into halves

1 cup diced jicama

½ cup chopped red bell pepper

1 head red leaf lettuce, torn into bite-size pieces

½ cup lightly salted peanuts, chopped

Combine mayonnaise, cumin, lemon juice, onion powder, salt, garlic powder and black pepper in small bowl. Blend well and set aside. Combine chicken, grapes, jicama and bell pepper in large bowl. Pour dressing over chicken mixture; stir well. Cover and refrigerate until chilled.

Line plates with lettuce and spoon chicken salad over top. Sprinkle with peanuts and serve immediately. *Makes 6 servings*

Grilled Tuna and Succotash Salad

1 cup uncooked dried baby
lima beans, rinsed
⅔ cup vegetable oil
¼ cup chopped fresh basil
3 tablespoons balsamic or
red wine vinegar
2 tablespoons Dijon mustard
2 tablespoons lemon juice
½ teaspoon salt
½ teaspoon black pepper

4 tuna steaks (about
6 ounces each)
1 cup frozen corn, thawed
2 large tomatoes, seeded and
chopped
Fresh arugula or spinach
leaves
Lemon slices and fresh dill
sprigs (optional)

Place beans in large saucepan; cover with 4 inches of water. Bring to a boil over high heat. Uncover pan; boil 2 minutes. Remove pan from heat; cover. Let stand 1 hour in water, then rinse and drain.

Combine oil, basil, vinegar, mustard, lemon juice, salt and pepper in glass jar with tight-fitting lid. Cover. Shake well; set aside.

Rinse tuna; pat dry with paper towels. Place tuna in shallow glass dish. Pour ¾ cup oil mixture over tuna. Coat tuna in mixture; cover and marinate in refrigerator 30 minutes.

Prepare grill for direct cooking. Transfer beans to large bowl. Add corn and tomatoes. Stir in remaining oil mixture. Cover; marinate at room temperature until ready to serve.

Drain tuna; discard marinade. Place tuna on grid. Grill over medium-high heat 6 to 8 minutes or until tuna flakes easily when tested with fork, turning halfway through grilling time.

Arrange tuna on arugula-lined plates. Spoon bean mixture over tuna. Garnish with lemon slices and dill, if desired.   *Makes 4 servings*

Grilled Tuna and Succotash Salad

Adobe Summer Salad

3 cups cooked converted white rice, chilled

2 cups diced red and/or yellow or orange bell peppers

1 can (15 ounces) black beans, rinsed and drained

1 tomato, chopped

1 cup diced jicama

1 cup diced cooked chicken or turkey breast

¾ cup sliced green onions

¼ cup chopped cilantro

1 cup thick and chunky salsa

2 tablespoons fresh lime juice

2 tablespoons vegetable oil

¼ teaspoon salt

8 large romaine lettuce leaves

Lime wedges (optional)

Combine rice, bell peppers, beans, tomato, jicama, chicken, green onions and cilantro in large bowl; mix well.

Combine salsa, lime juice, oil and salt in small bowl. Add to salad; toss well. (Salad may be served immediately or covered and chilled up to 8 hours before serving.) Serve salad over lettuce leaves with lime wedges, if desired.

Makes 6 servings

Orange Poppy Seed Salad

Honey & Poppy Seed Dressing (recipe follows)

Lettuce leaves

2 oranges, peeled and sliced crosswise

1 red onion, sliced and separated into rings

½ small jicama, cut into ½-inch strips

Prepare Honey & Poppy Seed Dressing; set aside.

Arrange lettuce leaves on serving plates; top with oranges, onion and jicama. Serve with dressing.

Makes 4 servings

Honey & Poppy Seed Dressing

½ cup mayonnaise

¼ cup sour cream or plain yogurt

2 tablespoons honey

1 tablespoon lemon juice

1 teaspoon poppy seeds

Whisk together all ingredients. (Dressing may be thinned with a few tablespoons milk, if desired.)

Makes ¾ cup

Creamy Coconut-Lime Fruit Salad

½ cup sour cream
½ cup unsweetened coconut
  milk
2 tablespoons lime juice
2 tablespoons brown sugar
2 seedless oranges, peeled
  and sectioned

2 Granny Smith apples, cored
  and chopped
2 ripe nectarines, pitted and
  sliced
1 ripe mango, peeled, pitted
  and diced
1 cup strawberry halves

Combine sour cream, coconut milk, lime juice and brown sugar in small bowl; stir until smooth. Gently toss remaining ingredients in large bowl. Pour sour cream mixture over fruit. Toss to coat well. Serve immediately or cover and refrigerate up to 4 hours. *Makes 6 to 8 servings*

Marinated Antipasto

1 cup julienne-sliced carrots
1 cup fresh green beans, cut
  into 2-inch pieces
1 cup fresh brussels sprouts,
  quartered
1 cup thinly sliced baby
  yellow squash
1 can (9 ounces) artichoke
  hearts, drained, quartered
½ cup thinly sliced red bell
  pepper
½ cup thinly sliced yellow
  bell pepper

2 cups water
½ cup white wine vinegar
1 tablespoon olive oil
1 teaspoon sugar
2 bay leaves
1 clove garlic
6 sprigs fresh thyme
¼ teaspoon black pepper
½ cup chopped green onions
  with tops
½ cup minced parsley
  Peel of 2 oranges, cut into
  thin strips

Bring 4 cups water to a boil in large saucepan over high heat. Add carrots, beans, brussels sprouts, squash, artichoke hearts and bell peppers; cover and simmer 1 minute or until vegetables are crisp-tender. Remove from heat; drain. Place in heatproof bowl.

Combine 2 cups water, vinegar, oil, sugar, bay leaves, garlic, thyme and black pepper in medium saucepan. Bring to a boil over medium heat. Pour over vegetables; mix well. Cool completely. Cover and refrigerate 12 hours or up to 3 days before serving.

Before serving, drain vegetables. Discard bay leaves, garlic and thyme. Toss vegetables with onions, parsley and orange peel.

Makes 8 servings

Thai Grilled Beef Salad

3 tablespoons Thai
   seasoning, divided
1 pound beef flank steak
1 tablespoon finely chopped
   lemongrass
2 red Thai chilies or 1 red
   jalapeño pepper, seeded
   and sliced into thin
   slivers
2 tablespoons chopped
   cilantro

2 tablespoons chopped fresh
   basil
1 tablespoon minced red
   onion
1 tablespoon fish sauce
   Juice of 1 lime
1 clove garlic, minced
1 carrot, grated
1 cucumber, chopped
4 cups assorted salad greens

Prepare grill for direct grilling.

Sprinkle 1 tablespoon Thai seasoning over beef; turn to coat. Cover and marinate 15 minutes. Grill beef 5 to 6 minutes per side or until desired doneness is reached. Cool 10 minutes.

Meanwhile, combine remaining 2 tablespoons Thai seasoning, lemongrass, chilies, cilantro, basil, onion, fish sauce, lime juice and garlic in medium bowl; mix well.

Thinly slice beef across grain. Add beef, carrot and cucumber to dressing; toss to coat. Arrange on bed of greens.   *Makes 4 servings*

Spinach-Melon Salad

6 cups torn stemmed washed
   spinach
4 cups mixed melon balls,
   such as cantaloupe,
   honeydew and/or
   watermelon
1 cup sliced zucchini
½ cup sliced red bell pepper

¼ cup thinly sliced red onion
¼ cup red wine vinegar
2 tablespoons honey
2 teaspoons olive oil
2 teaspoons lime juice
1 teaspoon poppy seeds
1 teaspoon dried mint leaves

Combine spinach, melon balls, zucchini, bell pepper and onion in large bowl.

For dressing, combine vinegar, honey, oil, lime juice, poppy seeds and mint in small jar with tight-fitting lid; shake well. Pour over salad; toss gently to coat.   *Makes 6 servings*

Smoked New Potato Salad

2 cups hardwood chips
  Dill Vinaigrette (recipe
  follows)
2 pounds new potatoes
1 yellow or red bell pepper,
  halved

1 tablespoon olive oil
2 tablespoons (1 ounce)
  crumbled feta cheese

Cover hardwood chips with water and soak for at least 30 minutes. (If using wooden or bamboo skewers, prepare by soaking in water 20 to 30 minutes to keep from burning.) Prepare Dill Vinaigrette; set aside.

Place potatoes in large saucepan and cover with water; bring to a boil over high heat. Reduce heat to medium and simmer 8 to 10 minutes or until crisp-tender; drain and cool. (Potatoes can be prepared ahead and refrigerated for up to one day.)

Grill bell pepper halves skin-side down on covered grill over medium coals 15 to 25 minutes or until skin is charred, without turning. Remove from grill and place in plastic bag until cool enough to handle, about 10 minutes; remove pepper skin with paring knife and discard. Chop pepper; set aside.

Halve potatoes and place in medium bowl. Drizzle with oil; stir to coat potatoes evenly. Spray hinged wire grill basket with nonstick cooking spray. Place potatoes in basket, arranging in single layer; close securely. (Or, thread potatoes onto 5 or 6 prepared skewers.) Drain hardwood chips and sprinkle over hot coals. Grill potatoes on covered grill over medium to hot coals 12 to 16 minutes (6 to 10 minutes if using skewers) or until golden, turning once. Remove to serving bowl; add bell pepper and gently stir in dressing. Sprinkle with cheese; gently combine. Garnish as desired.

Makes 6 servings

Dill Vinaigrette

¼ cup thinly sliced green
  onions
2 tablespoons chopped fresh
  dill weed

2 tablespoons rice vinegar or
  cider vinegar
1 tablespoon Dijon mustard
1 tablespoon olive oil

Whisk all ingredients together in small bowl.   *Makes about ½ cup*

Spicy Grapefruit Salad with Raspberry Dressing

2 cups washed watercress
2 cups washed mixed salad greens
3 grapefruit, peeled, sectioned and seeded
½ pound jicama, cut into julienne strips

1 cup fresh or thawed frozen raspberries
2 tablespoons chopped green onion
1 tablespoon honey
1 teaspoon balsamic vinegar
½ to ¾ teaspoon dry mustard

Combine watercress and salad greens; divide between 4 salad plates. Arrange grapefruit and jicama on top of greens.

Reserve 12 raspberries for garnish. For dressing, combine remaining raspberries, green onion, honey, vinegar and mustard in food processor or blender; process until smooth. Drizzle dressing over salads; garnish with reserved raspberries.

Makes 4 servings

Summertime Vegetable Salad

2 tablespoons butter or margarine
3 cups canned diced tomatoes, drained
1 zucchini, halved and sliced

2 cups fresh or thawed frozen whole kernel corn
⅓ cup chopped onion
¼ teaspoon ground black pepper

Melt butter in large nonstick skillet over medium-high heat. Add tomatoes, zucchini, corn, onion and pepper. Cook 5 minutes or until vegetables are tender, stirring occasionally. Serve warm or cover and refrigerate until ready to serve.

Makes 6 servings

Coca-Cola®

JUST ADD COKE®

Uncle Joe's Baked Beans

8 slices bacon, cut into
    ½-inch pieces
1 onion, chopped
1 can (12 ounces)
    COCA-COLA®
1 can (6 ounces) tomato paste
1 tablespoon Dijon mustard
1 teaspoon hot pepper sauce

1 can (15 ounces) kidney
    beans, drained
1 can (15 ounces) pinto
    beans, drained
2 cans (8 ounces each)
    crushed pineapple,
    drained

Cook bacon and onion over medium-high heat in large skillet until bacon is browned and crispy. Drain fat; set aside.

Preheat oven to 375°F. Spray 13×9-inch casserole with nonstick cooking spray.

Meanwhile, combine COCA-COLA®, tomato paste, mustard and hot pepper sauce in large bowl; mix well. Add beans, pineapple and bacon mixture to COCA-COLA® mixture; mix well. Transfer to prepared dish. Bake, uncovered, 20 to 25 minutes or until beans are hot and bubbly.

Makes 4 to 6 servings

Marinated Pork Tenderloin

1 cup COCA-COLA®
¼ cup beef broth
2 tablespoons cider vinegar
1 tablespoon honey mustard
2 small Granny Smith apples, chopped
4 to 6 green onions, finely chopped
2 cloves garlic, minced
1 teaspoon ground cinnamon
½ teaspoon ground ginger
Salt and black pepper to taste
1 to 1½ pounds whole pork tenderloin

Combine COCA-COLA®, beef broth, vinegar and mustard in large bowl; mix well. Add apples, onions, garlic, cinnamon, ginger, salt and black pepper to COCA-COLA® mixture; mix well.

Place pork tenderloin in large plastic resealable food storage bag. Pour mixture over pork, turning to coat. Seal bag and marinate in refrigerator at least 3 hours to let flavors blend, turning occasionally.

Preheat oven to 350°F. Remove pork from marinade; discard marinade. Place pork in roasting pan. Cook pork 25 to 30 minutes or until internal temperature reaches 165°F when tested with meat thermometer inserted into thickest part of pork.

Remove pork from oven and transfer to cutting board. Let stand 10 to 15 minutes before carving. Internal temperature will continue to rise 5° to 10°F during stand time. Serve with applesauce and your favorite side dishes.

Makes 4 to 6 servings

40

TIP

Pork tenderloin is exactly what it sounds like: the most tender cut of meat from the loin. It is a strip of meat that lies along each side of the backbone.

Italian-Style Vegetable Soup

1 package (12 ounces)
uncooked small pasta
shells or corkscrew pasta

1 can (28 ounces) crushed
tomatoes in purée

2 cups water

1 can (15 ounces) white
beans, rinsed and
drained

1 can (14½ ounces)
vegetable broth

1 can (12 ounces)
COCA-COLA®

2 cloves garlic, minced

1 bay leaf

2 teaspoons Italian
seasoning blend

1 teaspoon salt

½ teaspoon white pepper

1 bag (16 ounces) frozen
vegetable medley, such
as broccoli, green beans,
carrots and red bell
peppers

Juice of ½ lemon

Cook pasta according to package directions; drain. Set aside.

Combine tomatoes, water, beans, broth, COCA-COLA®, garlic and bay leaf in large Dutch oven. Add seasoning blend, salt and white pepper; mix well. Bring to a boil over high heat. Reduce heat to low and simmer 10 to 15 minutes, stirring occasionally.

Add frozen vegetables to Dutch oven and return to a boil over high heat. Stir in pasta and reduce heat to low. Simmer 10 to 15 minutes or until heated through. Remove bay leaf; stir in lemon juice. Ladle soup into bowls. Garnish, if desired. Serve immediately.   *Makes 6 to 8 servings*

42

TIP

A good soup pot is one that is heavy and conducts and distributes heat evenly. Copper is the ideal metal, though its cost puts it out of the range from most cooks. Good alternatives are aluminum or stainless steel with a copper or aluminum core.

Chocolate COKE® Cake with Chocolate Cream Cheese Frosting

1 box (18¼ ounces)
chocolate cake mix
1 cup COCA-COLA®
½ cup vegetable oil

¼ cup water
3 eggs
Chocolate Cream Cheese
Frosting (recipe follows)

Preheat oven to 350°F. Grease 13×9-inch cake pan.

Combine cake mix, COCA-COLA®, oil, water and eggs in large bowl. Beat at low speed of electric mixer until blended; beat at medium speed 2 minutes. Pour batter into prepared pan. Tap pan several times on countertop to release air bubbles.

Bake 30 to 35 minutes or until toothpick inserted into center of cake comes out clean. Cool in pan on wire rack 10 minutes. Remove from pan to wire rack; cool completely. Place cake on serving plate and frost top with Chocolate Cream Cheese Frosting. Garnish, if desired.

Makes 12 servings

Chocolate Cream Cheese Frosting

4 cups powdered sugar, sifted
⅓ cup unsweetened cocoa
powder
1 package (8 ounces) cream
cheese, softened

½ cup (1 stick) butter, softened
1 teaspoon vanilla extract

Combine sifted powdered sugar and cocoa in large bowl; set aside.

Beat cream cheese, butter and vanilla in large bowl until smooth. Gradually fold in powdered sugar mixture into cream cheese mixture.

Makes about 1½ cups frosting

TIP

Save yourself lots of time in the kitchen and substitute canned chocolate (or any flavor) frosting for the frosting recipe.

Coca-Cola®

44

Asian Beef Stir-Fry

1½ pounds flank steak, cut into ⅛-inch strips then into 1½-inch pieces

1 can (12-ounces) COCA-COLA®

1 cup beef broth

3 tablespoons soy sauce

1 teaspoon sesame oil

2 cloves garlic, minced

3 tablespoons peanut oil, divided

1 yellow bell pepper, cut into thin strips

1 red bell pepper, cut into thin strips

4 green onions, sliced diagonally

1 cup water chestnuts

1 tablespoon cornstarch

2 cups hot cooked rice

Place steak in large resealable plastic food storage bag. Add COCA-COLA®, beef broth, soy sauce, sesame oil and garlic; seal bag and turn to coat. Marinate at least 3 hours or overnight in refrigerator, turning occasionally.

Remove steak from bag; reserve half of marinade in medium bowl. Heat wok or skillet over high heat until hot. Drizzle 2 tablespoons peanut oil into wok; heat 30 seconds. Add half of steak; stir-fry 2 minutes or until beef is browned and no longer pink. Repeat with remaining steak; set aside.

Reduce heat to medium-high and add remaining 1 tablespoon peanut oil; heat 30 seconds. Add bell peppers, onions and water chestnuts; cook and stir 3 minutes or until vegetables are tender. Remove and set aside.

Stir cornstarch into reserved marinade until smooth. Stir marinade into wok and boil 1 minute, stirring constantly. Return beef and vegetables to wok; cook 3 minutes or until heated through. Serve over rice.

Makes 4 servings

Peanutty COKE® Cow

1 cup COCA-COLA®
½ teaspoon cherry extract or
    1 teaspoon maraschino
    cherry liquid
2 scoops vanilla ice cream

2 teaspoons dry-roasted
    peanuts, finely chopped
2 maraschino cherries, sliced
    in half

Pour COCA-COLA® into large drinking glass; stir in cherry extract. Place vanilla ice cream in another large glass; add peanuts and cherries. Pour COCA-COLA® mixture over ice cream mixture. Serve immediately.

Makes 1 serving

Cherry and COKE® Apple Rings

3 Granny Smith or other tart
    apples, peeled and cored
½ teaspoon plus ¼ teaspoon
    sugar-free cherry-
    flavored gelatin

⅓ cup COCA-COLA®
⅓ cup non-dairy whipped
    topping

Slice apples crosswise into ¼-inch-thick rings. Place stacks of apple rings in large microwavable bowl; sprinkle with gelatin. Pour COCA-COLA® over rings.

Cover loosely with waxed paper. Microwave at HIGH 5 minutes or until liquid is boiling. Allow to stand, covered, 5 minutes. Arrange on dessert plate. Serve warm with whipped topping.   *Makes 3 to 4 servings*

TIP

Crisp, tart, juicy Granny Smith apples are not only delicious eaten raw, but are also excellent for cooking because they keep their texture.

48

Country Captain Chicken

¼ cup olive oil

4 boneless skinless chicken breast halves

1 onion, sliced

1 green bell pepper, sliced

1 can (14½ ounces) chicken broth

1 cup COCA-COLA®

1 can (14½ ounces) whole tomatoes, undrained and coarsely chopped

1 can (6 ounces) tomato paste

1 teaspoon hot pepper sauce

½ teaspoon ground white pepper

1 bay leaf

2 tablespoons chopped parsley

2 cups hot cooked rice

Heat oil in large skillet over medium-high heat. Add chicken breasts; cook 3 to 4 minutes on each side or until lightly browned. Remove from skillet, set aside.

Add onion and bell pepper to skillet. Cook and stir 5 minutes or until vegetables are tender. Add chicken broth and COCA-COLA® to skillet, scraping up any browned bits from bottom of pan. Add tomatoes, tomato paste, hot pepper sauce, white pepper and bay leaf. Cook and stir 5 minutes or until sauce thickens slightly. Return chicken to pan and simmer, uncovered, about 15 minutes or until chicken is no longer pink in center.

Remove chicken breasts to serving platter. Remove and discard bay leaf. Pour sauce over chicken and garnish with chopped parsley. Serve with hot cooked rice.

Makes 4 servings

Creamy Caribbean Shrimp Salad

1 cup mayonnaise
¼ cup cocktail sauce
¼ cup **COCA-COLA**®
1 teaspoon lime juice
½ teaspoon salt
¼ teaspoon ground black pepper
1 pound shrimp, cooked and cleaned

1 package (10 ounces) prepared mixed salad greens
2 ripe mangoes, peeled, pitted and sliced
½ cup chopped walnuts

Combine mayonnaise, cocktail sauce, COCA-COLA®, lime juice, salt and black pepper in small jar with tight fitting lid. Shake well. Refrigerate until ready to use.

Combine shrimp, salad greens, mangoes and walnuts in large bowl. Divide mixture onto plates. Drizzle dressing over salads.   *Makes 4 servings*

TIP

Varying in size, shape and color, the yellowish orange flesh of the mango has a rich flavor and a spicy aroma. Mangoes must be fully ripe before eating or using in recipes. Allow them to ripen at room temperature until soft, then use or refrigerate for a few days.

52

Hickory Smoked Barbecued Chicken Wings

2 pounds chicken wings, tips removed, cut in half

3 teaspoons hickory flavor liquid smoke, divided

1 cup barbecue sauce

1 cup COCA-COLA®

⅓ cup honey

¼ cup ketchup

2 teaspoons spicy mustard

2 teaspoons hot pepper sauce

1 teaspoon Worcestershire sauce

¼ cup sliced green onions (optional)

Place chicken wings in large resealable plastic food storage bag; add 2 teaspoons liquid smoke. Toss to coat; refrigerate at least 1 hour to let flavors blend.

Preheat oven to 375°F. Spray 13×9-inch baking pan with nonstick cooking spray.

Combine barbecue sauce, COCA-COLA®, honey, ketchup, mustard, hot sauce, Worcestershire sauce and remaining 1 teaspoon liquid smoke in medium bowl; mix well. Pour sauce into prepared pan. Add chicken wings to pan; toss to coat.

Bake 35 to 40 minutes or until chicken is tender and no longer pink, basting occasionally with sauce and turning once. Remove pan from oven and discard sauce, leaving just enough to coat wings. Set oven to broil and return wings to oven. Broil 3 to 4 minutes. Garnish with green onions, if desired, just before serving. *Makes about 24 appetizers*

COKE® Chili

1 pound ground beef
1 onion, chopped
4 ribs celery, chopped
1 can (15 ounces) tomato
   sauce
1 can (14½ ounces) beef
   broth
2 tablespoons chili powder
1 teaspoon garlic powder

1 teaspoon paprika
1 teaspoon ground cumin
1 can (15 ounces) kidney
   beans, drained
1 cup COCA-COLA®
1 teaspoon hot pepper sauce
1 teaspoon unsweetened
   cocoa powder
Salt and black pepper

Spray 3-quart Dutch oven with nonstick cooking spray. Cook beef, onion and celery over medium-high heat until meat is browned and vegetables are tender. Drain excess fat.

Add tomato sauce, beef broth, chili powder, garlic powder, paprika and cumin to meat mixture; stir well. Bring to a boil over high heat. Reduce heat and let simmer, uncovered, 20 minutes, stirring occasionally.

Stir in beans, COCA-COLA®, hot pepper sauce and cocoa powder. Continue to simmer 10 to 15 minutes. Season to taste with salt and black pepper. Garnish with sour cream and shredded cheese, if desired. Serve immediately. *Makes 4 to 6 servings*

56

TIP

Unsweetened cocoa is formed by extracting most of the cocoa butter from pure chocolate and grinding the remaining chocolate solids into a powder. In recipes, do not substitute sweetened cocoa, the type that is used for making hot chocolate, for unsweetened cocoa.

Mixed Fruit Compote

1 cup COCA-COLA®
1 cup water
¾ cup orange juice
½ teaspoon almond extract
1 can (21 ounces) cherry
    pie filling

1 can (16 ounces) sliced
    peaches, drained
1 cup dried cranberries
    Mint leaves (optional)

Combine COCA-COLA®, water, orange juice and almond extract in large saucepan; mix well. Stir in pie filling, peaches and cranberries.

Bring fruit mixture to a boil over medium-high heat. Reduce temperature to low and simmer 12 to 15 minutes or until fruit is tender. Serve warm, at room temperature or chilled. Garnish with mint leaves, if desired.

Makes 6 servings

TIP

To make orange juice from a partially used can of concentrate, measure the amount of remaining concentrate and then add 3 times that amount in water. Stir well and enjoy.

Coca-Cola®

BURGERS!
BURGERS!
BURGERS!

Hawaiian-Style Burgers

1 ½ **pounds ground beef**
⅓ **cup chopped green onions**
2 **tablespoons Worcestershire**
 sauce
⅛ **teaspoon black pepper**

⅓ **cup pineapple preserves**
⅓ **cup barbecue sauce**
6 **pineapple slices**
6 **hamburger buns, split and**
 toasted

Combine beef, onions, Worcestershire sauce and pepper in large bowl. Shape into six 1-inch-thick patties.

Combine preserves and barbecue sauce in small saucepan. Bring to a boil over medium heat, stirring often.

Place patties on grill rack directly above medium coals. Grill, uncovered, until desired doneness, turning and brushing often with sauce. Place pineapple on grill; grill 1 minute or until browned, turning once.

To serve, place patties on buns with pineapple.   *Makes 6 servings*

Middle Eastern Vegetable Grain Burgers

⅓ cup uncooked dried red lentils, sorted and rinsed

¼ cup uncooked brown or basmati rice

1 tablespoon olive oil

1 pound fresh mushrooms, sliced

1 onion, chopped

¾ cup grated Parmesan cheese

½ cup walnut halves, finely chopped

¼ cup chopped fresh cilantro

2 eggs

½ teaspoon black pepper

6 toasted sesame seed buns or toasted pita bread halves

Mayonnaise

Sliced red onion

Shredded lettuce

Sliced tomatoes

Place lentils in medium saucepan; cover with 1 inch water. Bring to a boil; reduce heat to low. Simmer, covered, 25 to 35 minutes or until tender. Rinse, drain and set aside. Meanwhile, cook rice according to package directions; set aside.

Heat oil in heavy large skillet over medium heat. Add mushrooms and chopped onion. Cook and stir 20 to 25 minutes or until mushrooms are brown. Combine mushroom mixture, cheese, walnuts, lentils, rice, cilantro, eggs and pepper in large bowl; mix well. Cover; chill.

Preheat broiler. Grease 15×10-inch jelly-roll pan with oil. Shape lentil mixture into 6 (½-inch-thick) patties. Arrange patties on prepared pan. Broil, 4 inches from heat, 3 to 4 minutes on each side or until golden brown, turning once. Serve on buns with mayonnaise, red onion, lettuce and tomatoes.

Makes 6 servings

Middle Eastern Vegetable Grain Burger

Blue Cheese Burgers

1¼ pounds lean ground beef
1 tablespoon finely chopped onion
1½ teaspoons chopped fresh thyme or ½ teaspoon dried thyme leaves
¾ teaspoon salt
Dash ground black pepper
4 ounces blue cheese, crumbled

Prepare grill for direct cooking.

Combine ground beef, onion, thyme, salt and pepper in medium bowl; mix lightly. Shape into 8 patties.

Place cheese in center of four patties to within ½ inch of outer edge; top with remaining patties. Press edges together to seal.

Grill 8 minutes or to desired doneness, turning once. Serve with lettuce, tomatoes and Dijon mustard on whole wheat buns, if desired.

Makes 4 servings

Grilled Salsa Turkey Burger

3 ounces lean ground turkey
1 tablespoon mild or medium salsa
1 tablespoon crushed baked tortilla chips
1 ounce sliced reduced-fat Monterey Jack cheese (optional)
1 whole wheat hamburger bun, split
1 lettuce leaf
Additional salsa

Combine turkey, 1 tablespoon salsa and chips in small bowl; mix lightly. Shape into patty. Lightly oil grid rack to prevent sticking.

Grill over medium-hot coals 6 minutes on each side or until no longer pink in center, turning once. Top with cheese during last 2 minutes of cooking time, if desired. Place bun, cut sides down, on grill during last 2 minutes of cooking time to toast until lightly browned.

Cover bottom half of bun with lettuce; top with burger, additional salsa and top half of bun.

Makes 1 serving

Blue Cheese Burger

Mexicali Burgers

Guacamole (recipe follows)
1 pound ground beef
⅓ cup salsa or picante sauce
⅓ cup crushed tortilla chips
3 tablespoons finely chopped cilantro
2 tablespoons finely chopped onion
1 teaspoon ground cumin

4 slices Monterey Jack or Cheddar cheese
4 kaiser rolls or hamburger buns, split
Lettuce leaves (optional)
Sliced tomatoes (optional)

To prevent sticking, spray grid with nonstick cooking spray. Prepare coals for grilling. Meanwhile, prepare Guacamole.

Combine beef, salsa, tortilla chips, cilantro, onion and cumin in medium bowl until well blended. Shape mixture into 4 burgers. Place burgers on grid, 6 inches from medium coals. Grill, covered, 8 to 10 minutes for medium or until desired doneness is reached, turning once. Place 1 slice cheese on each burger during last 1 to 2 minutes of grilling. If desired, place rolls, cut-side down, on grid to toast lightly during last 1 to 2 minutes of grilling. Place burgers between rolls; top burgers with Guacamole. Serve with lettuce and tomatoes, if desired. Garnish as desired.

Makes 4 servings

Guacamole

1 ripe avocado, pitted and peeled
1 tablespoon salsa or picante sauce

1 teaspoon lime or lemon juice
¼ teaspoon garlic salt

Place avocado in medium bowl; mash with fork until avocado is slightly chunky. Add salsa, lime juice and garlic salt; blend well.

Makes about ½ cup

Mexicali Burger

Lentil Burgers

1 can (about 14 ounces) defatted low-sodium chicken broth*

1 cup dried lentils

1 small carrot, grated

¼ cup coarsely chopped mushrooms

1 egg

¼ cup dry unseasoned bread crumbs

3 tablespoons finely chopped onion

2 to 4 cloves garlic, minced

1 teaspoon dried thyme leaves

Nonstick cooking spray

¼ cup plain nonfat yogurt

¼ cup chopped seeded cucumber

½ teaspoon dried mint leaves

¼ teaspoon dried dill weed

¼ teaspoon black pepper

⅛ teaspoon salt

Dash hot pepper sauce

To defat chicken broth, skim fat from surface of broth with spoon. Or, place can of broth in refrigerator at least 2 hours ahead of time. Before using, remove fat that has hardened on surface of broth.

Bring chicken broth to a boil in medium saucepan over high heat. Stir in lentils; reduce heat to low. Simmer, covered, about 30 minutes or until lentils are tender and liquid is absorbed. Let cool to room temperature.

Place lentils, carrot and mushrooms in food processor or blender; process until finely chopped but not smooth. (Some whole lentils should still be visible.) Stir in egg, bread crumbs, onion, garlic and thyme. Refrigerate, covered, 2 to 3 hours.

Shape lentil mixture into four ½-inch-thick patties. Coat large skillet with cooking spray; heat over medium heat. Cook patties over medium-low heat about 10 minutes or until browned on each side.

For sauce, combine yogurt, cucumber, mint, dill, black pepper, salt and hot pepper sauce in small bowl. Serve sauce over burgers.

Makes 4 servings

Mediterranean Burgers

1½ pounds ground beef
¼ cup (1 ounce) shredded
   mozzarella cheese
2 tablespoons grated
   Parmesan cheese
2 tablespoons chopped
   kalamata olives

1 tablespoon chopped fresh
   parsley
1 tablespoon diced tomato
2 teaspoons dried oregano
   leaves
1 teaspoon black pepper
4 hamburger buns, split

Prepare grill for direct cooking.

Shape beef into eight ¼-inch-thick burger patties.

Combine cheeses, olives, parsley, tomato, oregano and pepper in small bowl. Place ¼ cheese mixture on top of 1 burger patty; spread to within ½ inch of edge. Top cheese mixture with another burger patty; seal edge to enclose filling. Repeat with remaining cheese mixture and burger patties.

Place burgers on grid. Grill, covered, over medium heat 8 to 10 minutes for medium or until desired doneness is reached, turning halfway through grilling time.

Remove burgers from grill. Place burgers between buns.

Makes 4 servings

Bacon Burgers

1 pound lean ground beef
4 crisply cooked bacon slices,
   crumbled
1½ teaspoons chopped fresh
   thyme or ½ teaspoon
   dried thyme leaves

½ teaspoon salt
   Dash freshly ground pepper
4 slices Swiss cheese

Prepare grill for direct cooking.

Combine ground beef, bacon, thyme, salt and pepper in medium bowl; mix lightly. Shape into 4 patties.

Grill 4 minutes; turn. Top with cheese. Continue grilling 2 minutes or to desired doneness.

Makes 4 servings

Fresh Rockfish Burgers

8 ounces skinless rockfish or scrod fillet
1 egg white *or* 2 tablespoons egg substitute
¼ cup dry bread crumbs
1 green onion, finely chopped
1 tablespoon finely chopped parsley
2 teaspoons fresh lime juice
1½ teaspoons capers

1 teaspoon Dijon mustard
¼ teaspoon salt
⅛ teaspoon black pepper
Nonstick cooking spray
4 grilled whole wheat English muffins
4 leaf lettuce leaves
4 slices red or yellow tomato
Additional Dijon mustard (optional)

Finely chop rockfish and place in medium bowl. Add egg white, bread crumbs, onion, parsley, lime juice, capers, 1 teaspoon mustard, salt and pepper; gently combine with fork. Shape into 4 patties.

Spray heavy grillproof cast iron skillet or griddle with nonstick cooking spray; place on grid over hot coals to heat. Spray tops of burgers with additional cooking spray. Place burgers in hot skillet; grill on covered grill over hot coals 4 to 5 minutes or until burgers are browned on both sides, turning once. Serve on English muffins with lettuce, tomato slices and additional mustard, if desired.   *Makes 4 servings*

Backyard Burgers

1½ pounds ground beef
⅓ cup barbecue sauce, divided
2 tablespoons finely chopped onion

½ teaspoon dried oregano leaves
6 onion hamburger buns, split and toasted

In large bowl, combine ground beef, 2 tablespoons barbecue sauce, onion and oregano. Shape into six 1-inch-thick patties.

Place patties on grill rack directly above medium coals. Grill, uncovered, until desired doneness, turning and brushing often with remaining barbecue sauce. To serve, place patties on buns.   *Makes 6 servings*

Fresh Rockfish Burger

Deviled Burgers

2 slices bread, finely chopped
¼ cup finely chopped onion
¼ cup ketchup
1 tablespoon Worcestershire
    sauce
2 teaspoons mustard
2 teaspoons creamy
    horseradish

½ teaspoon garlic powder
½ teaspoon chili powder
1 pound extra-lean ground
    beef
6 hamburger buns

Preheat broiler. Combine bread, onion, ketchup, Worcestershire sauce, mustard, horseradish, garlic powder and chili powder in large bowl until well blended. Gently blend ground beef into mixture. (Do not overwork.)

Shape mixture into 6 (3-inch) burgers. Place burgers on *ungreased* jelly-roll pan.

Broil burgers 4 inches from heat source 4 minutes per side or until desired doneness. Serve on hamburger buns. Garnish, if desired.

Makes 6 servings

Spicy Burrito Burgers

6 tablespoons mild salsa,
    divided
1 can (4 ounces) diced green
    chilies, divided
¼ cup sour cream
    Dash hot pepper sauce

1 pound ground beef
4 (6-inch) flour tortillas
1 cup shredded lettuce
½ cup (2 ounces) shredded
    Cheddar cheese with
    taco seasonings

Combine 2 tablespoons salsa, 2 tablespoons chilies, sour cream and hot pepper sauce in small bowl; set aside.

Combine beef, remaining 4 tablespoons salsa and remaining chilies in large bowl; mix well. Shape into four 4-inch oval patties.

Grill burgers over medium coals 8 to 10 minutes for medium or until desired doneness is reached, turning halfway through grilling time.

Place 1 burger in center of 1 tortilla. Top with one-quarter of lettuce, cheese and sour cream mixture. Bring edges of tortilla together over top of burger; secure with toothpick if necessary. Repeat with remaining burgers. Remove toothpick before serving.

Makes 4 servings

Mini Burgers

1 pound ground chicken
¼ cup Italian-style dry bread
    crumbs
¼ cup chili sauce
1 egg white
1 tablespoon white
    Worcestershire sauce
2 teaspoons Dijon mustard
½ teaspoon dried thyme
    leaves
¼ teaspoon garlic powder

32 thin slices plum tomatoes
    (about 3 medium)
½ cup sweet onion slices
    (about 1 small)
16 slices cocktail rye or
    pumpernickel bread
Mustard (optional)
Pickle slices (optional)
Snipped chives or green
    onion tops (optional)

Preheat oven to 350°F. Combine chicken, bread crumbs, chili sauce, egg white, Worcestershire sauce, mustard, thyme and garlic powder in medium bowl. Form mixture into 16 patties.

Place patties in 15×10-inch jelly-roll pan. Bake, uncovered, 10 to 15 minutes or until patties are no longer pink in centers.

Place 2 tomato slices and 1 onion slice on each bread slice. Top each with 1 patty; add dollops of mustard, pickle slices and chives, if desired.

Makes 16 appetizer servings

Scandinavian Burgers

1 pound lean ground beef
¾ cup shredded zucchini
⅓ cup shredded carrots
2 tablespoons finely minced
    onion
1 tablespoon fresh chopped
    dill *or* 1 teaspoon dried
    dill weed

½ teaspoon salt
¼ teaspoon black pepper
1 egg, beaten
¼ cup beef broth

Prepare grill for direct cooking.

Combine ground beef, zucchini, carrots, onion, dill, salt and pepper in medium bowl; mix lightly. Stir in egg and beef broth. Shape into 4 patties.

Grill 8 minutes or to desired doneness, turning once. Serve on whole wheat buns or rye rolls, if desired.

Makes 4 servings

Southwest Pesto Burgers

CILANTRO PESTO

1 large clove garlic

4 ounces fresh cilantro, stems removed and rinsed

1½ teaspoons bottled minced jalapeño pepper *or* 1 tablespoon bottled sliced jalapeño pepper, drained

¼ teaspoon salt

¼ cup vegetable oil

BURGERS

1¼ pounds ground beef

¼ cup plus 1 tablespoon Cilantro Pesto, divided

½ teaspoon salt

4 slices pepper jack cheese

2 tablespoons mayonnaise

4 kaiser rolls, split

1 ripe avocado, sliced

Salsa

For pesto, with motor running, drop garlic through feed tube of food processor; process until minced. Add cilantro, jalapeño pepper and salt; process until cilantro is chopped.

With motor running, slowly add oil through feed tube; process until thick paste forms. Transfer to container with tight-fitting lid.

Prepare barbecue grill for direct cooking.

Combine beef, ¼ cup pesto and salt in large bowl; mix well. Form into 4 patties. Place patties on grid over medium-hot coals. Grill, uncovered, 4 to 5 minutes per side or until meat is no longer pink in center. Add cheese to patties during last 1 minute of grilling.

While patties are cooking, combine mayonnaise and remaining 1 tablespoon pesto in small bowl; mix well. Top patties with mayonnaise mixture. Serve on rolls with avocado and salsa.   *Makes 4 servings*

Southwest Pesto Burger

Greek Lamb Burgers

¼ cup pine nuts
1 pound lean ground lamb
¼ cup finely chopped onion
3 cloves garlic, minced,
    divided
¾ teaspoon salt
¼ teaspoon black pepper
¼ cup plain yogurt

¼ teaspoon sugar
4 slices red onion
    (¼ inch thick)
1 tablespoon olive oil
8 pumpernickel bread slices
12 thin cucumber slices
4 tomato slices

Prepare grill for direct cooking. Meanwhile, heat small skillet over medium heat until hot. Add pine nuts; cook 30 to 45 seconds or until light brown, shaking pan occasionally.

Combine lamb, pine nuts, chopped onion, 2 cloves garlic, salt and pepper in large bowl; mix well. Shape mixture into 4 patties, about ½ inch thick and 4 inches in diameter. Combine yogurt, sugar and remaining 1 clove garlic in small bowl; set aside.

Brush 1 side of each patty and onion slice with oil; place on grid, oiled sides down. Brush tops with oil. Grill, on covered grill, over medium-hot coals 8 to 10 minutes for medium or to desired doneness, turning halfway through grilling time. Place bread on grid to toast during last few minutes of grilling time; grill 1 to 2 minutes per side.

Top 4 bread slices with patties and red onion slices; top each with 3 cucumber slices and 1 tomato slice. Dollop evenly with yogurt mixture. Top sandwiches with remaining 4 bread slices. Serve immediately.

Makes 4 servings

TIP

Pine nuts are actually seeds that grow inside the cones of several varieties of pine trees. Purchase pine nuts in health food stores, nut shops or larger supermarkets. Store pine nuts in a plastic bag or airtight container and refrigerate up to 3 months or freeze up to 9 months.

Greek Lamb Burger

76

Coca-Cola®

TOO HOT TO BAKE

Fresh Fruit Trifle

2 cups fat-free (skim) milk
2 tablespoons cornstarch
⅓ cup sugar
4 egg whites, lightly beaten
2 teaspoons vegetable oil
1½ teaspoons vanilla
6 tablespoons apple juice, divided

4 cups cubed angel food cake
6 cups diced assorted fruit (apricots, peaches, nectarines, plums and berries)

Combine milk and cornstarch in medium saucepan; stir until cornstarch is dissolved. Add sugar, egg whites and oil; mix well. Bring to a boil over medium-low heat, stirring constantly with wire whisk; boil until thickened. Remove from heat. Cool. Add vanilla and 2 tablespoons apple juice.

Place one-third cake pieces in bottom of 2-quart glass bowl or trifle dish. Sprinkle with one-third remaining juice. Spoon ⅔ cup custard over cake. Spoon one-third fruit over custard. Repeat process twice, ending with fruit. Serve immediately. *Makes 12 servings*

Watermelon Ice

4 cups seeded 1-inch
    watermelon chunks
¼ cup thawed frozen
    unsweetened pineapple
    juice concentrate

2 tablespoons fresh lime juice
Fresh melon balls
    (optional)
Fresh mint leaves
    (optional)

Place melon chunks in single layer in plastic freezer bag; freeze until firm, about 8 hours. Place frozen melon in food processor container fitted with steel blade. Let stand 15 minutes to soften slightly. Add pineapple juice and lime juice. Remove plunger from top of food processor to allow air to be incorporated. Process until smooth, scraping down sides of container frequently. Spoon into individual dessert dishes. Garnish with melon balls and mint leaves, if desired. Freeze leftovers. *Makes 6 servings*

Honeydew Ice: Substitute honeydew for the watermelon and unsweetened pineapple-guava-orange juice concentrate for the pineapple juice concentrate.

Cantaloupe Ice: Substitute cantaloupe for the watermelon and unsweetened pineapple-guava-orange juice concentrate for the pineapple juice concentrate.

Note: Ices may be transferred to airtight container and frozen up to 1 month. Let stand at room temperature 10 minutes to soften slightly before serving.

80

Frozen Peanut Butter-Banana Dessert

2 large ripe bananas, cut into
    ½-inch slices
½ cup no-sugar-added
    natural peanut butter
    (creamy or chunky)

½ cup half-and-half

Place bananas in single layer in plastic freezer bag; freeze until firm, at least 8 hours. Combine peanut butter and half-and-half in food processor container fitted with steel blade; cover and process until smooth. Add frozen bananas; let stand 10 minutes to soften slightly. Process until smooth, scraping down sides of container frequently. (Dessert will be soft-set.) Serve immediately or cover and freeze in airtight container until serving time. Freeze leftovers. *Makes 4 servings*

Note: Place frozen dessert in refrigerator 15 to 20 minutes before serving or let stand at room temperature 10 minutes before serving to soften slightly.

Watermelon Ice, Cantaloupe Ice and Honeydew Ice

Frozen Strawberry Pie

3 tablespoons margarine
2 tablespoons honey
1½ cups crushed pretzels
3 cups low-fat sugar-free strawberry frozen yogurt, softened
1½ cups light nondairy whipped topping, thawed

2 teaspoons grated lime peel, divided
1 package (16 ounces) strawberries in syrup, thawed
1 tablespoon lime juice

Combine margarine and honey in medium microwavable bowl. Microwave at HIGH 30 seconds or until smooth when stirred. Add pretzels; stir until evenly coated. Press onto bottom and side of 9-inch pie plate; freeze 30 minutes or until firm.

Combine frozen yogurt, whipped topping and 1 teaspoon lime peel in medium bowl; gently fold with rubber spatula or wire whisk. Spoon into pie plate. Freeze 2 hours or until firm.

Combine strawberries, lime juice and remaining 1 teaspoon peel in small bowl; stir to blend.

Cut pie into 8 portions; serve with strawberry mixture.

Makes 8 servings

Berried Cantaloupe with Honey Dressing

Honey Dressing (recipe follows)

2 small cantaloupes
2 cups raspberries

Prepare Honey Dressing; cover. Refrigerate.

Cut cantaloupes in half; remove seeds. Cover; refrigerate.

When ready to serve, place cantaloupe halves in individual bowls; fill centers with raspberries. Drizzle with dressing. *Makes 4 servings*

Honey Dressing

1 cup plain yogurt
2 tablespoons honey

2 teaspoons grated orange peel

Combine all ingredients; mix until well blended.

Makes about 1 cup

Fruit Freezies

1½ cups (12 ounces) canned or thawed frozen peach slices, drained
¾ cup peach nectar

1 tablespoon sugar
¼ to ½ teaspoon coconut extract (optional)

Place peaches, nectar, sugar and extract in food processor or blender container; process until smooth.

Spoon 2 tablespoons fruit mixture into each section of ice cube tray.

Freeze until almost firm. Insert frill pick into each cube; freeze until firm.

Makes 12 servings

Apricot Freezies: Substitute canned apricot halves for peach slices and apricot nectar for peach nectar.

Pear Freezies: Substitute canned pear slices for peach slices, pear nectar for peach nectar and almond extract for coconut extract.

Pineapple Freezies: Substitute crushed pineapple for peach slices and unsweetened pineapple juice for peach nectar.

Mango Freezies: Omit coconut extract. Substitute chopped fresh mango for canned peach slices and mango nectar for peach nectar.

84

TIP

You can also pour ⅓ cup fruit mixture into each of 8 plastic pop molds or small paper or plastic cups. Freeze until almost firm. Insert wooden stick into each mold; freeze until firm. Makes 8 servings.

Chocolate Raspberry Mousse Pie

**6 ounces bittersweet or
semisweet chocolate,
chopped and divided**
**¼ cup plus 2 tablespoons
seedless raspberry jam,
divided**

**4 cups thawed frozen
whipped topping, divided**
**1 (9-inch) prepared chocolate
cookie crumb pie crust**
**1 pint fresh raspberries,
divided**

Place 4 ounces chocolate in microwavable bowl. Microwave at HIGH 1 to 1½ minutes. Stir in 3 tablespoons jam until melted. Cool to room temperature.

Gently fold ½ cup whipped topping into chocolate mixture until blended. Fold 1½ cups whipped topping into mixture. Spoon into pie crust and refrigerate.

Fold remaining 2 cups whipped topping into remaining 3 tablespoons jam. Fold in half of raspberries. Spread mixture over chocolate layer. Cover and refrigerate at least 6 hours.

Place remaining 2 ounces chocolate in microwavable 1-cup measure. Microwave at HIGH about 1 minute. Stir until smooth; drizzle over pie. Top with remaining raspberries. *Makes 8 servings*

Tip: For a special touch, garnish the top of the pie with a slice of kiwi.

Mango Vanilla Parfait

**½ (4-serving size) package
vanilla sugar-free instant
pudding mix**
1¼ cups fat-free (skim) milk
½ cup mango cubes
2 large strawberries, sliced

**3 sugar-free shortbread
cookies, crumbled or
2 tablespoons reduced-
fat granola**
**Strawberry slices for
garnish**

Prepare pudding according to package instructions using 1¼ cups milk.

In parfait glass or small glass bowl, layer one-quarter of pudding, half of mango, half of strawberries and one-quarter of pudding. Repeat layers in second parfait glass. Refrigerate 30 minutes.

Just before serving, top with cookie crumbs and garnish with additional strawberries. *Makes 2 servings*

Berry Delicious Trifles

1 package (4-serving size)
   instant vanilla pudding
   and pie filling mix
2¼ cups milk
1 cup sliced strawberries
1 cup raspberries
1 cup blueberries

1 frozen pound cake
   (10¾ ounces), thawed
2 tablespoons orange juice
¼ cup orange marmalade
Sweetened whipped cream
   and mint leaves
   (optional)

Beat pudding mix and milk in medium bowl with electric mixer at low speed 2 minutes; set aside. Combine strawberries, raspberries and blueberries in medium bowl; set aside.

Slice cake into 12 slices, each about ½-inch wide. Brush one side of each piece with orange juice; spread marmalade over juice.

Cut cake slices in half lengthwise. Place 4 pieces of cake each against side of 6 martini or parfait glasses with marmalade side toward center of glass.

Place ¼ cup berries in bottom of each glass; top each with heaping ⅓ cup pudding mix and then ¼ cup berries. Refrigerate 30 minutes. Garnish with sweetened whipped cream and mint leaves, if desired.

Makes 6 servings

Marinated Pineapple Dessert

1 can (20 ounces) pineapple
   chunks in juice,
   undrained
2 tablespoons honey
1 stick cinnamon, broken in
   pieces

1 tablespoon lemon juice
1 teaspoon vanilla
½ teaspoon grated lemon peel
1½ cups strawberries, cut into
   halves, or blueberries
¼ cup toasted flaked coconut*

To toast coconut, spread on baking sheet. Bake in preheated 300°F oven 4 to 6 minutes or until light golden brown, stirring frequently. Remove from pan to cool.

Combine pineapple with juice, honey, cinnamon, lemon juice, vanilla and lemon peel in small saucepan. Bring to a boil over medium-high heat. Pour mixture into medium bowl; refrigerate, covered, at least 4 hours or up to 24 hours.

Drain pineapple mixture; reserve liquid. Remove cinnamon pieces. Arrange pineapple and strawberries in 4 dessert dishes. Pour reserved liquid over fruit. Sprinkle with coconut before serving.

Makes 4 servings

Strawberry Charlotte

4 fresh strawberries, sliced
⅔ cup plus 3 tablespoons sugar, divided
1 teaspoon unflavored gelatin
1 package (6-serving size) vanilla pudding mix
2½ cups reduced-fat (2%) milk
1 package (16 ounces) frozen unsweetened strawberries, thawed, undrained

3 cups frozen whipped topping, thawed, divided
⅔ cup chopped fresh strawberries or whole fresh blueberries
1 package (7 ounces) dry Champagne biscuits (4-inch-long ladyfinger-like biscuits)

Line bottom and side of 5-cup soufflé dish with heavy-duty plastic wrap. Arrange sliced strawberries in bottom of prepared dish. Set aside.

Bring ⅔ cup water and ⅔ cup sugar to a boil in small saucepan, stirring constantly, until sugar melts. Remove from heat; cool.

Combine gelatin and 1 tablespoon water in small bowl. Combine pudding mix and milk in heavy saucepan. Cook and stir over medium heat until mixture comes to a boil. Remove from heat. Add gelatin to pudding mixture; stir until gelatin dissolves. Transfer mixture to large bowl; cool slightly.

Place frozen strawberries in food processor or blender; process until smooth. Stir ½ cup strawberry purée into pudding mixture; let stand 15 to 20 minutes or until cool but not set, stirring occasionally. Gently fold 2½ cups whipped topping and chopped strawberries into pudding mixture.

Trim about 15 biscuits to 3-inch lengths. Dip into sugar mixture, allowing excess to drip back into saucepan. Arrange biscuits around side of prepared dish, sides touching and rounded ends pointing up. Spoon pudding mixture into prepared dish. Dip remaining biscuits in sugar mixture, allowing excess to drip back into saucepan; arrange on top of pudding mixture. Cover and refrigerate overnight.

Stir remaining 3 tablespoons sugar into remaining strawberry purée; cover and refrigerate overnight. To complete recipe, unmold charlotte onto serving platter; remove plastic wrap. Serve with strawberry purée and remaining ½ cup whipped topping.   *Makes 6 servings*

Serving Suggestion: Serve with additional fresh strawberries or blueberries.

Caramel Sundae

1 cup low-fat (1%) milk
1 tablespoon cornstarch
½ cup firmly packed dark
   brown sugar
1 tablespoon margarine

1 teaspoon vanilla
1 pint vanilla ice milk or
   nonfat frozen yogurt,
   divided

Combine milk and cornstarch in heavy saucepan. Stir until cornstarch is completely dissolved. Add brown sugar and margarine; cook over medium-low heat, stirring constantly with wire whisk. Bring to a boil. Boil 1 minute. Remove from heat; stir in vanilla. Cool to room temperature.

Place ½ cup ice milk in each of 4 dishes. Top each with ¼ cup caramel sauce.

Makes 4 servings

Cheesecake Parfaits

1 envelope unflavored gelatin
¼ cup fat-free (skim) milk
1 container (16 ounces)
   1% low-fat cottage
   cheese
1 container (8 ounces) lemon
   low-fat yogurt, divided

¼ cup sugar
¼ teaspoon salt
4 tablespoons graham
   cracker crumbs, divided
   Strawberries for garnish
   (optional)

Sprinkle gelatin over milk in small saucepan; let stand 1 minute to soften. Cook and stir constantly over low heat until gelatin dissolves, about 3 to 5 minutes. Remove from heat; cool slightly.

Add cottage cheese, ½ cup yogurt, sugar and salt to food processor; process until combined. With motor running, slowly add gelatin mixture; process until combined. Spoon ½ tablespoon crumbs into each of 4 large dessert glasses or wine glasses. Spoon an equal amount of cottage cheese mixture into each glass; sprinkle with another ½ tablespoon crumbs. Cover and refrigerate about 2 hours or until firm. Just before serving, top each parfait with spoonful of remaining yogurt. Garnish with strawberries, if desired.

Makes 4 servings

Fruit Tray with Honey-Lime Sauce

1 cantaloupe, seeded and peeled

1 papaya, seeded and peeled

1 small fresh pineapple, peeled, cored and cut into triangles or short spears

1½ cups strawberries, hulled, or 6 fresh figs, cut into halves

2 kiwifruit, peeled and thinly sliced

1 cup (½ pint) whipping cream

3 tablespoons honey

1 teaspoon grated lime peel

2 teaspoons lime juice

2 bananas

Mint sprig for garnish

Cut cantaloupe and papaya into ½-inch crescents. Arrange cantaloupe, papaya, pineapple, strawberries and kiwifruit on large serving platter. Cover and chill up to 4 hours. Whip cream in medium bowl until soft peaks form. Fold in honey, lime peel and lime juice. Cover and refrigerate 2 hours for flavors to blend.

To serve, slice bananas crosswise; arrange on fruit platter. Spoon whipped cream mixture into serving bowl; serve with fruit. Garnish with mint.

Makes about 8 servings

Papaya Pops

1 very ripe papaya

1 cup peach or vanilla low-fat yogurt

2 tablespoons honey

¾ teaspoon grated lime peel

1 teaspoon lime juice

Cut papaya lengthwise into halves; discard seeds. Scrape out flesh with spoon; discard skin. Combine papaya, yogurt, honey, lime peel and lime juice in blender or food processor. Blend until smooth.

Fill four 5-ounce paper or pliable plastic kitchen cups with papaya mixture. Freeze 20 minutes. Insert wooden ice cream stick or plastic spoon in center of each cup. Freeze 8 hours or overnight until firm.

To serve, peel away paper cup or gently twist and ease frozen pop out of plastic cup.

Makes 4 servings

92